Reverse Psychology:
The Dirty little secrets that you wish you knew

By Katherine Shepard

Table of Contents

Chapter One

Analyzing Different types of Personality

The personality of an individual is decisions they take throughout their life using the experiences of their complete life. This decision plays a very crucial role in deciding one's personality. There are various factors like natural, genetic, and environmental that are responsible for the development of one's personality. According to process, "personality also colors our values, beliefs, and expectations.

Many other factors like hereditary factors that also contribute a lot to personality development have been established because of interactions with the social environment. Personalities are the sum total of individual's Psychological traits, motives, attitudes, habits, beliefs, characteristic and outlooks.

Personality is different ways in which an individual interacts and reacts with others. Personality by definition can also be generally as the deep ingrained and relative enduring patterns of feeling, behavior and thought. While referring to personality it is, the characteristics that make one stand out in a crowd. it generally implies uniqueness of an individual.

It is said that: If greater success, improved and self-esteem and happiness are your life destination, the power of positive habits can take a person towards its goal. Personality development is a simple but powerful program that can transform any life.

Personality is totality what a person do, reacts, and interacts with others. Personality is a thought, feeling and behavior and its combination. It is something unique to an individual that make him different in the crowd.

Personality Development includes Self-improvement, Building leadership and positive attitude, positive personality development, Human resource development, creative intelligence, CEO guide, Brainstorming etc.

Personality development may also include power of positive habits, ultimate brainpower, and conversation confidence, the lasting happiness and success formula, conversation confidence, shyness and social anxiety system etc.

In other word personality development is technique for building self-confidence, Gaining positive leadership quality, learning the techniques for positive attitude, and using self-esteem techniques in positive sense.

A character's personality refers to his/her appearance, traits, mindset, mindset and behavior with others. This can also be referred to as personality Enhancement education or personality Enhancement course.

Allow us to undergo the importance of Personality development Training:

personality development grooms an individual and enables him to make a mark of his/her own. Individuals need to have fashion in their personal for others to comply with them. Do no longer blindly reproduction others. You want to set an instance for human beings around. Personality development not only makes you appearance accurate and presentable however additionally allows you face the arena with a grin.

Personality improvement is going a protracted way in lowering stress and conflicts:

It encourages people to look at the brighter facets of existence. Face even the worst conditions with a smile. Agree with me, flashing your trillion-dollar smile will no longer most effective soften half of your problems however also evaporate your pressure and worries. There is no factor cribbing over minor issues and issues.

Personality development facilitates you increase a tremendous mindset in lifestyles:

A character with a poor mindset finds a hassle in each scenario. Instead of cribbing and criticizing human beings around, analyze the complete situation and try to find the perfect solution for the same. Remember, if there may be a problem, there must be a solution as properly. Never lose your cool. It might make the situation worse.

Personality development enables a character to inculcate tremendous traits like punctuality, flexible mindset, willingness to learn, friendly nature, eagerness to assist others and so forth.

By no means, hesitate to share information with others. Always reach office on time. A few human beings will be inclined to paintings until late. Late sittings no longer simplest increase your pressure levels however additionally damages your private life. Sitting until overdue at the workplace shows that an individual is extraordinarily bad in time control abilities.

There are four personality types, fire, wind, water and ice. The one that you will motivate with the great lifestyle network marketing companies give you will be the fire. The ones who will enjoy the opportunity to talk to many people about the business will be the wind. Those who will enjoy having the opportunity to help other people are your water; and those who will conduct their businesses in perfect order will be the ice. Once you figure which personality type you are engaging with you can become a chameleon and be more like that person. How do you know which personality type is the person in?

You can spot these personality types by looking at them. The fire types are very flashy and will be wearing the expensive jewelry and clothes and driving expensive cars. If you see anyone who is dressed in a manner that they stand out in the crowd that will, most likely, be your wind type. These women wear the most makeup and have a tendency to dye their hair. They also are a very touchy-feely type of people so the person whom you notice is hugging and touching everyone may be the wind type. Those who are completely focused on others are the type who will not try to call too much attention to themselves so anyone you see who fits that description and is not wearing a lot of makeup may be a water type. To find your ice types you will need to look for the conservatively dressed people who are not out to show off how much money they make.

You can determine which of the personality types you are dealing with even if you are not seeing the person. There are several questions you can be asked that will give you the clues you need. Ask them what job they are currently doing. If you find out that they are in a profession that doesn't tie them up in a cubicle and allows for a lot of change you might have a fire. If the person is in a customer service-driven profession you may have found someone who likes to talk a lot and is wind. If the person is in a helping profession it is likely that you have found a water type. Someone who is in an analytical profession may be an ice type.

The next question should be to find out how long the prospect has been doing his current job. The answer you might be looking for is one that tells you the prospect has been in the current position a consistently long time, which may mean there is a perfect personality match. Supposing that you are talking to a younger person, you can ask them how they came to be in the job they are in; the answer will give your insight into the personality of that person if she explains why she thought her current job would be a good one for her.

It is imperative that you learn the personality types intimately before you begin prospecting in a network marketing business. They tell you a lot about the person and what will or will not work, when pitching a business opportunity. You will thrive with the presentation your company gives you with the fire and the wind types, but you will fall flat on your face if you present to the water and ice the same way. Lucky for you, you have had some personality training and you know that prospecting the same way to everyone regardless of personality type will not build you the type of down line you desire.

The personality test is one of the tests that are taken to define a person's character, which might be shown or exposed within the person's lifetime. This defines the individuals' character and pattern of thoughts, feelings and behavior. This type of test can be scored by using a dimensional or typological approach. Dimensional approaches to the Big 5 test such as the NEO-PIR can define personality as a group of continuous dimension wherein individuals differ and can be very powerful.

Typological approaches like the Myers-Briggs Type Indicator define opposing categories of functioning wherein individuals differ. There are also normative responses for every category can be graphed as normal curves that can imply that some aspects of the personality of some people are better than others.

Meanwhile, the Ipsative test can offer two equal

responses where an individual can choose. These responses can result in bi-modal graphs. Meanwhile personality test like the strength deployment inventory assesses purpose or motivation of behavior. It is known that three continuums of purpose which are combined to yield seven distinct types.

On the other hand, emotive tests could become unreliable because the test taker can try to pick the answer that they feel would best fit their ideal self so they end up answering the test untruthfully so the result might not be correct.

Every meaning of a personality test scores can be difficult to interpret in a direct sense. That is the reason why producers of personality test make ample efforts to produce norms that can provide a comparative basis to interpret a test taker's test scores. The common format for the norms is the percentile ranks, then scores and percentile ranks.

However, there are certain controversies that surround these kinds of tests. One of them is that the test taker will only find the result accurate because if the validation of the subjects involved. This is where the taker will only recognize the information that will apply to him.

Another is the application of the test for non-clinical purposes. Some companies are intrigued in administering these tests to their employees as often as a psychiatric patient's experience, which is not acceptable. Another problem is the test taker is faking everything. Test takers fake his answer to controlling the results.

Because of these, many strategies adopted to reduce the faking. One of these strategies involves giving the test taker a warning that there is a way to detect faking. This might result in a negative consequence to the test taker. Another is giving forced-choice item format. This requires the test taker to choose between substitutes of social desirability. Social desirability and lie scales can detect a certain pattern of responses. On the other side, one way to detect faking is by looking into the timing of each response on electronically administered tests.

Personality testing is used mostly in psychological researchers to test their different theories of personality. Researchers also show that some companies use personality testing as one of their hiring processes. However, some have been misused so some discontinued administering them.

Chapter-two

Kinesics and the Types of Gestures

Getting into the habit of reading body language has not always been an easy thing. Staring down people longer than socially acceptable may get you into to trouble but as you get more advanced, reading people will become as easy as speaking your native language.

Kinesics, or body language, refers to the subconscious gestures and body movements we make. They denote what someone is thinking or feeling. Since these gestures are made subconsciously, it is difficult to fake your body language. However, it is not completely impossible to do so.

The practical application of kinetics can be separated into two categories:

Interpretation of body language Manipulation of your own body language

Interpreting body language simply means reading a person's gestures and ascertain what the gestures indicate. Has the person lied to you? Was he uncomfortable about what you were talking about?

While manipulating body language means to consciously alter your body language. What can you do to look like you have more confidence? What can you do to attract the opposite sex? To manipulate your body language, you will need to, first know how to read body language. After all, how can you alter what you do not understand?

Generally, most people do not mean what they say. There is a contrast between what people say and what they actually mean. According to research the impact of what you say is 7%, how you say it, i.e. voice modulation, tone and so on is 38% and the remaining 55% is body language.

Are not the statistics interesting? What is so prominent about non-verbal communication? Why is it given such importance?

Body Talk

There are two parts in communication; the verbal and the non-verbal. The latter, generally referred to as body language. Does the body have a language? The answer is yes. There is a meaning in every body movement or gesture. According to the Oxford dictionary, a gesture is a movement of a part of the body to express an idea or meaning or an action made with one's feelings or intentions. It is a type of non-verbal communication performed by a body part, and used instead of or in a combination of verbal form of communication.

Body language is simply the outward reflection of a person's mental or emotional condition. Observing the body language of a person can convey a lot about him or her. It is given so much importance because actions speak louder than words. The body doesn't know how to lie. Unconsciously, it will telegraph the thoughts as you fold your arms, cross your legs, stand, walk, move your eyes and your mouth.

Kinesics

Kinesics is the study of communication through body movements. It is a term developed by behaviorists to refer to the way various human gestures reflect feelings and attitudes. It was developed in the 1950s by an anthropologist known as, Dr.Ray L.Birdwhistell. He estimated that an average person speaks for a total of ten to twelve minutes a day and the time taken to complete the sentence is only 2.5 seconds.

Today, Kinesics is one of the most talked about and the most obvious non-verbal communication forms. It is also one of the most confusing areas of non-verbal communication behavior because there are various meanings that communicate through the same body movements across different races and cultures of the world.

This example will illustrate why the confusion prevails. The thumbs-up gesture when used may mean different things to different cultures. It means "good" in several Western cultures, "one" to Italians, and "five" to Japanese and is a rather rude gesture in Greek culture. Therefore, it could create a lot of confusion until one is well versed with the cultural influences and differences across the globe.

Kinesics categories are:

- Emblems
- Illustrators
- Affect displays
- Regulators
- Adapters.

Emblems are described as non-verbal messages, which have a verbal meaning. Illustrators are used to illustrating what is being said.

Affect Displays are body movements or facial expressions that show a person's emotional state.

Regulators are body movements or facial expressions that are used as means to continue a conversation. It can be used as a means to tell the other person that he/she is understood or simply it is used to give feedback.

Adapters are simple posture changes that may be needed so that the person may be comfortable.

Rules for Accurate Reading

The outcome of any given situation does not necessarily or directly reflect the attitude that a group of people or a person actually possess. Experts in the body language field always insist on some basic rules that should be adhered to. This is especially for beginners, so that they do not misinterpret what is actually happening.

Posture: Having the right posture is an important part of body language. It reflects your state of mind. Some simple tips are lean forward when listening and stand straight while speaking.

Gestures: Maintain a balance in the amount you gesture. B conscious of the gestures you are using in different situations and times. Do not overdo it, but you can still be expressive.

Shaking hands: Hands are a very important tool in body language. When shaking hands try to give as much pressure as the other person exerts. Holding the other person's hand limply or squeezing too hard is not advisable. Many times, it may cause people to develop negative feeling towards you.

Head movement: Head movement is important to maintain a rapport during a conversation. Some positive signs in body language are nodding the head while talking and tilting it when listening.

Territory: Territory is the amount of space occupied during a conversation. It'1s a good practice neither to stand too close nor too far while talking with people, particularly strangers.

The gesture is the movement of the body, head, arms and hands, together with facial expressions, to add emphasis and greater meaning to an idea or an emotion during an oral presentation or speech. It helps make a well-written and researched speech into a better-spoken presentation.

Below are some starting points you might consider allowing you to add gesture to your oral presentations.

Before you start to speak and/or gesture, have a neutral starting position - a stance without a gesture. This will give greater impact to your gesture.

- You must now let your hands be your friends when speaking. Do not leave them hanging by your side.

- Your gesture must be relevant to what you say.

- Use gesture to demonstrate or stress the idea/s you are suggesting.

- A gesture from the shoulder, not just the hands or wrists or from the elbow.

- Make your gestures a whole body experience.

- Your gestures must be expansive. Make sure you spread out your fingers to induce the expansiveness.

Leaning forward towards your audience at appropriate times in your speech can make the audience feel more included in what you are saying.

When you want to gesture, the brain, the voice and the body must be in tune with each other.

Learn to 'relax' your body. Nervousness curtails the impact of good gesture. Remember the audience is on your side. They want you to give a great speech.

After you have written and practiced your speech, plan where and what sort of gesture you will use. Often, the gesture will just occur naturally through the emotion of your words as you practice.

When you have decided where and what gestures you will use, print out your speech double spaced so that you can mark, in a different color, where and what gesture you will use. This will help you if you have a lectern and intend to use your written notes to deliver your speech.

You may need to use variations in pitch, loudness and the speed of your words to fit in with your gesture and the impact you want to produce in your audience.

Your body language must compliment your gesture, e.g. a smile may not go with a serious point you are making.

Do not shuffle, sway, or pace up and down and neither should one be immobile. These body movements will cause a loss of the visual impact that your gesture can add to your words.

It is important to ensure you do not have automatic gestures (mannerisms) that detract from what you are saying, i.e. meaningless and repetitive gestures. A neutral standing position will have less negative impact on the message of your speech than a gesture that is not related to the theme of the speech.

Remember that good gesture can add greater meaning and appeal to your speech. However, this can only truly happen if your speech is a good product. The great gesture will not rescue a poor speech. Just as writing a good speech is always a work in progress, so is creating the best gesture to go with each new speech you deliver.

Chapter Three

Common Hand Gestures and What They Mean

Let us start with the president himself. When he was doing his campaigns for the presidency in 2008 he was advised by his staff to change one of his gestures. He had a habit of pointing his index finger at the audience when he was making a point. Obama was advised to change that gesture to just holding up his index finger. What is the difference? In the first instance when he made a point, his finger was pointing at people, sending an unspoken message that he was blaming, scolding, or telling people what to do. Most people do not like anyone pointing fingers at them. In the new gesture, he holds up his finger to emphasize that he is making a point but no one feels blamed or singled out. You will probably never be in the position of giving speeches as tightly scripted and choreographed as this, but this story is certainly an example of the importance of non-verbal communication.

Our gestures are as important as our words when we are speaking. In fact, research shows that over half of our communication with others is non-verbal. Yet when new speakers step onto the podium they suddenly become self-conscious about their gestures and do not know what to do with their hands. This causes the speaker to look stilted. Because of this, it is important when you are practicing to consider the appropriate gestures that will accompany your words.

First, let us look at gestures and body language that need to be avoided when you speak. An easy way to see these is to make a video recording of yourself speaking. Play the video without sound. This makes your body language easy to see. It is painful to watch, but worth it!

Some of the body movements and gestures that are annoying or distracting to an audience. Some speakers roll back on their heels, sway or pace. Men have a tendency to jiggle their change in their pocket. Males and females both fiddle with rings, watches and other jewelry. In general, when you are speaking keep your hands away from your face and hair.

One of the most effective ways to eliminate these distracting mannerisms, in addition to videotaping yourself, is to ask a friend to keep track of them for you. Hearing how many times you repeat a particular gesture can make you much more aware of it. When you are trying to stop a particular behavior, it will cause you to be somewhat awkward when speaking. However, it will become natural with practice. Moreover, your audience will thank you!

I took a photography class from a young man who continually played with a plastic water bottle while instructing. He would take off the cap, take a quick sip, and recap the bottle and the make the plastic bottle "pop" by squeezing it. Then he would repeat the process- hundreds of times. I dearly wanted to take his water bottle away from him and throw it in the trash!

Any prospective speech benefits when you look at the entire package- your spoken words as well as your unspoken communication. a speaker can't get her message out effectively unless she is seen as sincere. If your words sound sincere but your mannerisms send a different message, your speech will fall flat.

I suggest you create your speech first and give it once looking in a mirror. See what gestures seem natural and spontaneous. Those natural gestures are what you want to keep in your speech. Do not use overblown gestures that seem phony. In addition, do not stand stiffly with your hands at your side. Do what feels natural.

The good news is that people's fears about what to do with their hands usually disappear once they get into their speech. They forget about their hands and their gestures become natural.

Gestures and body language can be very effective in reinforcing your points. Many people feel too self-conscious to watch themselves on tape. But, look at it this way. Everyone in your audience has to watch you so you might as well see how you are coming across to them!

Chapter four

Head Gestures

Head gestures allow people to communicate a variety of thoughts and feelings. However, head movements by themselves are incapable of being as precise as words. They are open to wide interpretations and many have multiple meanings. In many cases, the gesture's implications depend on the context of the scene, the dialogue, relationships, and the dramatic situation. As such, head gestures often embellish or accent what is actually being communicated by other dramatic choices.

The head's motions are numerous and include swivel, tilt, slant, or any combination thereof. They can also performed with varying qualities from accentuated to repressed, from fluid to frantic, from minimal to exaggerated. Another reason is their relationship to other acting entities such as dialogue, facial expressions and body movements. Do they precede, follow, or synchronize with these entities? Do they support or contradict the other entities portrayed? By exploring these aspects using various examples, you will better understand both the limits and potentials of head gestures.

Let us look at the most common gestures first. The nod of the head, tilting alternating up and down indicates agreement, acceptance, or acknowledgment. It could also mean, "Yes." The headshake, turning the head from side to side, is used often to mean "no." It is the most common form of expressing a negative reaction or indicating disagreement. These meanings, the nod and head shake, are accepted in much of the western world, however in some countries, other meanings prevail. For instance, in South Asian cultures, most notably India the side-to-side tilting of the head in arcs may mean "Yes', "Good", "OK" or "I understand" depending on the context.

The head toss could mean several things such as, "Get out of here", "It is over there", "Come over here," or "Shut up, the boss just came in." This gesture occurs mostly within group settings where a cryptic message must be conveyed. Thus, the head toss is usually subversive in nature, directed at one person and indicates a call to action. As such, eye contact with the recipient is required to complete the transaction.

The head roll has a number of interpretations such as, "I have no idea," "What could that be," or "Why are you asking me?" The gesture is also associated with avoidance of an issue with the roll directed away from the confronting person or entity. The eyes play a role in this interpretation, looking to areas devoid of people and their sight lines.

The cut-off is closely related to the head roll in that it indicates uncertainty or separation. This gesture consists of the head turning away from the confronting person and avoiding direct eye contact. The gaze may reflect an uncertainty or disagreement with eyes searching for answers and/or subtly commenting on the confronting person. The cut-off opens the door for unencumbered internalizations. No one is observing. In essence, a blocking move that allows another perspective of the character either portraying a truth or displaying deception.

Head up tilt may indicate contempt, a judgmental pose or "I'm better than you" stance. The accompanying facial expression can further define this gesture with flared nostrils for contempt, squinting eyes for the judgmental pose, and teetering head jiggle with a slight smile for superiority. The eyes clarify the target and the intensity can be varied to maintain interest. The gesture needs to be held long enough for appropriate impact. However, when held too long, the behavior becomes forced diminishing the integrity of the scene.

Side slant with the head leaning to one side can indicate interest, compassion, and even skepticism. When combined with searching eyes, interest becomes more evident. A downward tilt implies compassion when accompanied by sympathetic facial expressions. Skepticism becomes evident with side slant accompanied by a slight upward tilt and questioning eyes.

The Head Swivel has numerous applications. It can indicate what the character is talking or thinking about by the direction and target of the head turn. The "what" in these cases could be something tangible such as people or objects. They could also be imagined entities and the head turn combined with eye behavior takes us to that space. We see and feel what the character is visualizing. The head swivel is also used scanning and observing a new environment. Another application, when two people are conversing are side by side, the head swivel is used to acknowledge or comment on what is being said. When these subtle moves are incorporated into eye behavior, the exchange can be quite effective. This is because both behaviors are open to the audience and ideas, thoughts, and reflections become more important than the physical relationship.

The head swivel is also used in look always, detaching from the person you are talking to and turning to an internalization area. These areas include focal zones such as comfort area, problem area, recall, and avoidance areas. These areas combine head turns with eye behavior and help delineate areas of concern clarifying inner thoughts and feelings.

Around Corner. When something obstructs the character's view, the head moves to obtain a better angle. This movement incorporates the upper body moving sideways or up to get a better look. Such movement indicates a stronger commitment of interest than the side slant and increases the impact. This move can be done with only the upper body moving sideways or in combination with the head slant. The first is in the comic style while the latter is more realistic.

Emphatic Head Gestures can be used to evoke powerful feelings of convictions. Such movement, usually up and down, punctuates and emphasizes dialogue. Often these are synchronized with the rhythm and phasing of the words. However, when overused, the affect become redundant and looses impact. Yet, when properly placed and implemented, this gesture can be powerful tool in scenes having highly motivated speeches or confrontational arguments

Leaning in is indicative of being attentive, interested, or desirous. This head movement is usually very subtle and almost imperceptible, yet it has a telling affect on relationships. It signifies the person is actually listening. It implies a connection, either intellectual or emotional. When accompanied by appropriate facial expressions and eye behavior the viewer senses that is being communicated non-verbally. For instance, if the person leans in focusing longingly on her lips, it likely relates the emotion of desire.

Leaning back is indicative of being disinterested, cautious, or skeptical. This movement is usually reactionary and thus more perceptible. Something has come to change the demeanor of the character such as a boring subject, a precarious situation, or a worrisome proposition. The movement is one of survival and it implies a judgmental wait-and-see attitude. When abrupt, it might signify a scary or shocking event and set up flight or fight situation.

The Head Shrug has several meanings. It could imply that, "I do not know", "I do not care", "So what," or "Whatever". This movement raises the shoulders to shorten the neck. It can also incorporate a slanted head giving it a more congenial dimension. This gesture is sometimes used in combination with dialogue and implementing it before the dialogue is the most straightforward approach. This approach follows the feel-think-act-speak sequence. It is considered the most sincere. When implemented during the dialogue, the total effect is weaker. When inserted after the dialogue, the gesture could imply a reaction, intimidation or insincerity. It could also be an afterthought.

The Head Dip is a state of being associated with being tired, experiencing grief, or contemplating an idea or problem. Lowering the head allows the character to enter an area of comfort without distractions from others. As with all gestures, the juxtaposition with scene context, dialogue and facial expressions affect how one perceives the non-verbal entity.

The Crumble is a reactionary head movement, one that is often found in highly dramatic moments. The gesture combines the lean in with a subtle up and down quiver of the head as it moves forward. It is a gesture of expectation, relief, and sometimes grief. I call it the crumble as the character is almost falling apart as it dribbles forward and its vulnerability is most evident. This gesture is an internalization of both emotions and thoughts and as such, the target is what the character visualizes or imagines.

Eye/Nose Alignment is another aspect of head gestures. In conveying emotions such as suspicion and jealousy, the eyes move more acutely then do head movements. On the other hand, with emotions such as curiosity and desire, the eye/nose angle is more aligned. Likewise, in fearful situations, the eyes lead head movements and tend to be more acute. An acute eye/nose angle can also be used to show disdain or non-confrontational anger.

Stillness is another choice in head gestures. Minimal movements imply many things. It allows the eyes and facial expression to take center stage and do their thing. It also heightens tension and a feeling of vulnerability. By being motionless the viewer is allowed to enter the character's head and question what is going on inside. It also provides room for audience collaboration to speculate what is going to happen next.

Of the Flaws found in using head gestures, the most common is overuse. As with other gestures, when used repeatedly the effect wears off and the impact is lost. Instead, select key story moments where gestures will help support the character's emotions or intentions. In addition, rather than duplicating the dialogue content, seek out hidden facts that show the true essence of the scene. Find what is really going on, then use gestures to reveal them.

Another flaw is being too implicit, too on the nose. Here the gestures stand apart from the performance as highly noticeable elements impeding the integrity of the scene. Sometimes this fault has to do with not portraying the acting style correctly. For instance, in comic styles, the behavior is more exaggerated, precise and readable. In drama, the behavior is more credible, with implied meanings, and portrayed balancing the internal and external forces.

Being too mechanical is another common flaw, especially among beginners. Often this flaw can be corrected by practicing head gestures with varying intensities and speeds. Being able to control the qualities, timing, and dynamics should be a major part of your training as it allows for portrayals that are more authentic.

The dancing head flaw occurs where the head gyrates and this movement is not applicable to the character's behavior. This is usually an innate behavior of the actor and one of which he or she is not aware. This dancing head becomes apparent when the actor is required to rehearse with a book on one's head.

Other attributes. The head can also exhibit attitudes, opinions, and social status. For instance, an amicable attitude is going to more open and accommodating. A person with conservative opinions might be more uppity as opposed to the congenial stance of a liberal. Social status is also reflected in the lowered head of a suppressed sharecropper as opposed to a confident head-high pose of a company president.

The Size of Movement is another factor and dependent on the size of the head in the frame. When the head is relatively small as in a long shot, the movements have to be larger to have visual impact. In close up, the movements should be subtle, as they will appear larger and faster. On a theater stage, the same rationale applies and gestures have to be readable to the back seats.

Contradictions between head gestures and other acting choices are most infrequent. Normally gestures represent the truth while the dialogue, facial expressions, and blocking can represent a lie. Unscrupulous characters and con artists are sometimes betrayed by their truthful gestures while portraying a façade in other areas. This unsettling dissonance creates a deeper characterization that pulls the audience into the story. Conversely, a call girl might employ deceptive gestures to extract money from a client. These contradictions add color to the characters and make them more intriguing.

With movements and gestures, it is best to do less and make those actions stand out and be clearly readable. In addition, they should be in line with the story and consistent with the character and his or her relationships.

Writing about nonverbal entities and their implications is difficult in a literary format. Gestures are not word descriptions, they are movements expressing an idea or conveying a feeling. In visualizing these gestures, see them in motion with a beginning, middle, and end. In this way, you are more likely to express them in a fluid believable manner. Like all elements of acting, the goal should be to portray gestures in an organic and authentic way. This can be done through focused training and considerable practice to where they are generated instinctively as an integral part of the character's behavior.

As mentioned earlier, head gestures have multiple meanings and are shaped by the surrounding dramatics. This book explores some of these meanings; however, it cannot cover the many combinations available. One should pursue these possibilities and explore this subject on your own. People watching and studying award-winning performances are the best ways to assimilate the techniques outlined here. In your research, note the effective use of movements and gestures, and how using only what complements the dialogue and the telling of the story results in believable performances.

Chapter-five

Reading the Face

When I was a little girl my mom always said, "Do not make faces, you'll stay that way!" so with all honesty I'll have to admit that learning American Sign Language (ASL) was a real challenge for me. There was that fear that if I made facial contortions out of the ordinary that someday I would wake up with an abnormal facial expression that would never go away.

Not only making faces, but also culturally speaking touching oneself was another challenging aspect of learning American Sign Language.

Oh yes, and for the record, there is no such thing as a Universal Sign Language to date. There is however, American Sign Language, Mexican Sign Language, Japanese Sign Language, Chinese Sign Language, etc. I think you get the picture. For now let us place our attention on facial expressions which are very important communication components in ASL.

Facial expressions, when accompanied by Non-Manual Markers (NMM), are signals or gestures done without the use of the hands to relay a message. ASL Non-Manual Markers may include:

- Head tilt

- Shoulder raising

- Head nodding

- Brow raising

- Head shake

You probably use some type of sign language already and do not realize it. Here is an example:

Let us say you are in charge of a group of twenty children and you want them to be quiet. You would more likely signal your group in a fashion that carries your message by using an expressive look on your face. Maybe you would place your index finger over your mouth as a sign 'to hush'. If this did not get their attention, you would probably make it more expressive with the same gesture and an added wide-eyed expression making you look more serious. If this did not work, you may even place your hand on your hip, slightly bend at the waist, bring your index finger to your mouth in an exaggerated movement and furrow your brow. They would get the message for sure!

Well, that is just a tiny example of how facial expressions in ASL carry varied meanings in conversations. One very important note to make about facial expressions in ASL is the meaning behind the expression. In your effort to quiet the group of children above, did you notice that the added facial expressions had different meanings? Therefore, it is with ASL; facial expressions in American Sign Language may very well be used as an equivalent of vocal intonation in the hearing domain.

Moreover, here is the best part: ASL facial expressions have not changed my appearance as I was told when I was a child. I am certain they will not change yours either, (if you have pondered that fear too).

Harnessing the power and range of the face can be a challenging task for the actor. When we consciously think of these expressions, we are likely to produce false images. It is very hard to make the face behave upon command. However, there are ways to trick the brain and create believable expressions.

The ability to convey thoughts through facial expression is one of the humanity's greatest assets. Using the right one could be very advantageous for you as you are allowing those who are around you to understand you easily. This is not a learned ability or something that is brought about by the advancements of society since it is something that we naturally acquire as we grow and develop. Despite this, there are people who think that they could hide their emotions as they go about in their daily transactions with other people.

Most scientists and psychologist agree that there is only one noticeable feature in us that will give away our true emotions and this is our faces. So how do we detect the real emotions and intentions of those people around us using their facial expression? Experts agree that we could do so by understanding the true physiology of our faces and accurately identifying the several signatures each emotion brings to our faces.

It is all in the Face

As you may have known, the face is consists of a lot of muscles and nerves that will accurately display what we feel through facial expressions.

You must be able to identify the several telltale signs of each emotion as they can be obviously shown in the faces of other people. As this is an innate ability, every facial expression for each emotion is universal to all men no matter where they are in the world and in what culture they live in. With this in mind, several psychologists have listed several emotions and their facial signatures:

1. Sadness

This is usually characterized by dropping eyelids and the inner eyebrows being raised. The corner of the lips may also be lowered and the lips formed into a pout.

2. Happiness

One very telltale sign of this emotion is the corner of the mouth being lifted into a smile. The cheeks also rise as the outside corners of the brows are lowered.

3. Surprise

This emotion is made obvious when the upper eyelids and the eyebrows are raised. In most cases, even the jaws are dropped wide open.

4. Disgust

This emotion can be shown as the entire nose wrinkles as the upper lip is raised and the lower lip protrudes.

5. Anger

The entire face tightens while the brows are lowered and drawn together. Other signs include the jaws being pushed forward, the lips pressed together with the upper lip being raised a little.

6. Contempt

The only difference between anger and contempt is that the latter only affects one side of the face. This is characterized by a half of the upper lip being raised into a sneer.

7. Fear

This emotion generally characterized by the widening of the eyes and the dilating of the pupils. The lips are also stretched horizontally and there are also telltale signs of nervousness around the body like shaking or darting eyes.

Detecting a Person's Emotion

Fortunately, only the worst case of sociopaths can successfully hide their emotions and they make up for less than less than 1% of the world's population so any normal human being will not be successful in hiding their true feelings without being given away by their facial expression. You must first look at their eyes for this can show a lot of their hidden emotion. A person may be angry and may be hiding it behind polite words, wrinkling around the edges and the eyes open at half-mast will tell a very different story. Another example will be when a sad person tries to smile in public but is looking away, giving off their true feeling.

Another thing to look at when detecting a person's genuine emotion is their overall demeanor. Aside from facial expression, the things people subtly do while in public will give you clues on how they actually feel. For instance, truly happy people are characterized by a relaxed demeanor, coupled with a smile that is not forced. Also, unaffected and hands that are relaxed and open. Playing with the hair can also be a telltale sign of true happiness for women. People who hide their emotions, however, can be made obvious with a forced smile (a smile that looks rigid), clenched fists, closed arms signifying a defensive stance and very short responses when they are asked of a question. Aside from that, some tics like scratching and some verbal cues that people have will worsen when they are under stress.

Another thing to look for in their facial expression is when they overcompensate. Little children cannot help but smile when they lie thinking they might be getting away with it. Adult liars, on the other hand, will force themselves to look you in the eye to assure you of their "sincerity" or will try to avoid your eye contact altogether. In addition, there are people who often sneer when they talk to people they do not like, showing their contempt. Angry people often have overly intensive stares and a choice of words that can be described as unemotional and short due to the fact that they are trying their best not to blow up.

Chapter six

Proxemics, Posture, and Body Movements

The world in this day and age is obsessed with words. Many assume incorrectly that words make up the majority of interpersonal communication. In actual fact, 55% of communication is conveyed through body language and only 7% through words. It is worth considering that statistic for a moment. 55% of all communication is body language. With that fact, one thing is clear: for effective communication skills, you need good body language skills.

However, what are good body language skills? Body language can be used in myriad ways, from conveying confidence to attractiveness to friendliness and approachability. Here we shall examine a few of the best ways that body language can be used to improve the presentation of personality.

How to Use Good Body Language.

Conflict Resolution: Many are those who suffer from an unfortunate habit of getting into arguments for seemingly no reason. They do not say anything wrong, they are not aware of doing anything wrong, yet still, they keep getting into conflicts. The reason likely lies with their body language. They may have acquired negative body language gestures, such as crossing their arms across their chest, which can communicate negative, often aggressive feelings. These people can immediately improve the effectiveness of their communication through these simple do not:

* Avoid showing the lower teeth
* Do not fidget with the hair or face
* Avoid cross your arms over the chest
* Do not tap on objects
* Do not clench your fists

Good Dating Body Language:
There can be a little doubt that many people who begin to learn body language do so out of the desire to increase their success. Good for them. Body language is very effective stuff in dating. Here are

some ways to create the right image in dating through body language:

Smiling is a sign of submission. Use this body language gestures sparingly, but do use it. Stand with feet apart: Standing with your feet apart is a great gesture of confident body language. Just do not overdo it or you will look arrogant or aggressive. Show the palms of your hands when talking (obviously do so subtly). This helps one to build trust. Avoid crossing the arms or holding any object that might be in front of your body. This makes you less approachable.

Long Gazes: Long gazes are great for building intimacy

Mirror: Inconspicuously copies some of the body language gestures your target uses. This will make them feel significantly closer to you.
Take them to a number of different places while you are with them. This will make them feel as though they have known you longer (note: you do not need to go on holiday to do this. If you are in a club, spend

some time at the bar, some on the dance floor, some outside etc).

Friendliness:

Another great personality trait good body language can create is friendliness, which, believe it or not, is about a lot more than just smiling. To appear friendly:
- Do not hold your arms or any object in front of yourself
- Use your hands to gesture when speaking
- Smile occasionally
- Mirror the other person's body language
- Point your belly button and feet towards the other person. This shows interest in them.

These are just some of the things good body language can achieve. What is most important is that you recognize the power of body language and begin to be mindful of what your body language communicated. Just by opening your eyes to body language you'll learn a great deal and this will significantly help to improve the effectiveness of your communication.

Many individuals seem to falsely believe they can become more successful merely by being effective orators, and using compelling rhetoric and motivating. However, being a good orator is a positive asset. Most of the circumstances rhetoric alone cannot convince many people. Most people are evaluated more by their body language than by the content of their words, and this body language is often the result of a combination of professional training combined with integrity-based self-confidence.

1. Body language is a combination of many factors. These include posture, eye contact, eye movements how and where you place your arms and hands, and eye contact, gestures, etc. Do you slouch when you are with others, or are you standing erect? If you do not slouch, is your "good" posture stiff and erect, or relaxed and welcoming? Are your arms and hands relaxed, or do you, for example, fold your arms stiffly in front of you? How about your eyes? Are you directly at the individual, you speak to, or do you look away, to the side, etc.? How about your facial expression? Is it firm and unwelcoming, relaxed, or grinning all the time? Which would you feel most comfortable? Are you constantly gesturing, flailing

your arms about? Do you point directly at others, where your finger may give someone the feeling that it is almost weapon-like? Look in the mirror sometime and see what you do when you speak to others. Would you find your body language supportive, comforting and positive, or would it be a turn-off to you? It is important to think fully about the aura or mystique that you emit to others.

2. Your body language is often your graphic part of your presentation. Speakers in large forums use PowerPoint presentations or other visual aids to reduce the amount of attention from them alone. However, when you are in a situation where you are in a less formal setting, or without visual aids, a major part of the effectiveness of your presentation depends on the feeling others get from your body language. Is your body language positive or negative? Does it convey the same message that your words do?

Does one get the feeling from observing your body language that you are friendly, or do you appear standoffish. Does your body language transmit a message of integrity or not be trustworthy? Body language should be your ally and not your enemy. One can understand body language more clearly by reviewing both the televised tapes and the radio tapes of the 1960 Nixon-Kennedy debates. Most experts believe that if one only listened to the radio (in other words, only the words and even how they sounded), that Nixon won the debates.

However, these same experts believe that Kennedy overwhelming was the victor to those who watched on television, because of the appearance of both men, the difference in posture, the eye contact, the facial expression, etc. Undoubtedly, body language is something that most of us should spend more time understanding and enhancing, as well as focusing on making our body language consistent with the message we wish to convey.

We like to think that when we talk to others, that it is our words that convey the message to our audience, but what if I told you there was more to it than that? When people stop and listen to us, they not only listen - they are watching our body language - and sometimes our body language is telling a totally different story to what our words are saying!

It is known and factual that actions will always speak louder than words. You may say that you are keen as mustard to have that job and you tell the interviewer that you are confident and reliable. Your resume may even back you up. Nevertheless, if you fidget with your hair, cannot look them in the eye, and sit bolt upright with your arms tightly crossed - you are indicating that you are nervous, anxious and defensive. Not the image you may want to project when being interviewed for a job.

How you dress plus your mannerisms all add to the body language story you are telling. If your clothes are rumpled in any old color and combination, it says that you do not really care or respect yourself. That is fine if that is what you feel and if it is how you want to live. Nevertheless, if you want to get ahead in life, take the time to make sure your body language matches your words.

Tips to create a cool confident image when meeting and greeting new people is to walk into the meeting in a friendly confident way, make eye contact and give a firm but not bone-crunching handshake. Keep the limp fish handshake for a relative you do not like and want to annoy. Do not talk like a speeding train, and take a breath - let the other person get in a few words. Smile when appropriate, and keep movements to a minimum...do not fuss and fidget.

Do not tug your ears, fiddle with your cuff links, cross and uncross your legs, or fluff your hair- it can be distracting and indicates that you are uncomfortable. Even in this modern so-called enlightened age, women who smile too much at a male colleague flick their hair, and fiddle with the stem of a wine glass are indicating through body language that they are interested and available. No, it is not fair, but that is life. Therefore, watch that your body says if you want to avoid being hit on by Mr. Sleaze.

The best thing to do when talking to both new acquaintances and old is to give them the gift of your attention. There is nothing worse than talking to someone who is scanning the room in a bored stance as if looking for someone better than you to talk are. Be courteous and give them the attention they deserve. If you are stuck with the party bore, just make an excuse and politely move on.

Body language is overlooked often, but if you are aware of it, you can use it to your advantage in the workplace, home, and in building personal relationships. Body language tells more than your carefully crafted words can say, and if used the right way can get you up the ladder to success quicker than water down a drain pipe.

With a little bit of thought, you can use body language as a valuable tool for self-improvement and to leverage your way to your goals quicker.

Chapter seven

Four Simple Personality

Each of us are different in many ways and that fact cannot possibly be disputed by anyone who has any background in the human sciences, as it has been scientifically proven that we all have unique fingerprints, DNA, hair, looks, behavior and facial expressions and the combination of these things make us unique "personality types" so to speak. We also function from two different perspectives and we need to understand how each one of us functions. We each like to think that we are special (which we are) and in that portrayal system, we mostly portray what we perceive we want people to think about us. On the other side of the coin we have a reality in what we truly believe about ourselves and the way we feel inward. Many of us become disillusioned with our true inner picture, simply because of a misunderstanding of our personal purpose in life.

The fact that we allow this dissatisfaction to creep into our lives. We create an inner insecurity within ourselves. We then start looking at others or alternatively we start behaving like others, which is completely outside our true personality. Attempting to look different, behave different, think different, dress different and when looking at our big picture, become dissatisfied with our true personality, allowing society to name us as a "personality type" which is definitely going to influence our level to be successful in life. Society has made us believe that we need to conform to a standard of behavior, which then classifies us into various but different personality types, which seems impossible to escape from, due to the social pressures placed on society by those who wish to control our lives.

This type of personality manipulation is starting at a very young age in this modern time, where young boys or girls given labels, commonly known as Attention Deficit Disorder (ADD) or alternatively, Attention Deficit Hyperactive Disorder (ADHD). This immediately creates a personality label that have been proven through research conducted by the author and many other scholars, to be false and completely far from the true reality. The fact that each one of us is uniquely different and those different likes or dislikes and different beliefs between good and bad or alternatively right or wrong, and at the same time have many different talents in different areas. Should we be in school and have little interest in the subjects being taught, our attention span in the subject would be very short, making the ability to concentrate on the subject virtually impossible.

This does not mean that there is something wrong with us as unique individuals; it only means that we have no interest in the subject and therefore have nothing to motivate us in order to pay attention. We then start filling that time with some other activity to keep ourselves amused or occupied and more often than not disrupt the attention of others who have an interest in the subject. This behavior is then interpreted as a mental disorder of sorts namely, ADHD, which in reality is totally a false perception.

We consider such behavior as being disruptive. It would make a teacher's life difficult, however, that does not mean that our personality type is wrong. Therefore by creating such labels as being stupid, disobedient, impossible, lazy, et cetera, does not make our personality type, a mental disorder of any kind which was handed out by a third parties perception, who really does not have a clue what our real motivating fields of interest are at the outset.

These labels create a lot of inner insecurity as we are led to believe from the supposed experts that there is something radically wrong with us, creating a sense of feelings that are different to others making our behavior unacceptable and improper. Our self-perceptions are moved in such a way that we desire recognition for who we really are and we then start looking at others, who may have different areas of talents, creating a desire to be just like them.

These individuals are looked upon as "Stars" and a hero to envy. This leads us to attempt to look like them, and act like them, which is contradictory to our own personality. By trying to change those inner characteristics, which results in us becoming or entering into a state of disfunctionality, whereby our self-esteem degenerates while attempting to take on the personality of those perceived stars or personality types.

We will never be able to do that successfully unless we have the right personality values or talents that are similar to those stars. They lead us into creating escape mechanism such as smoking, drinking and or drugging, which seems to help us escape from the reality for a very short time. It eventually, results in us having to deal with the reality after a brief few hours once again. This results in a spiral decline in our ability to cope with acting out in a behavior or a personality which really is not who we are. This thereby inhibits our true personality to manifest itself, in order to live a truly satisfied and fulfilled lifestyle.

It is critical for each of us to understand our true unique inner talents and concentrate on those strengths and talents rather than being led into a trap, of being labeled as a personality type. Many millions of different individuals are struggling with their self-image and esteem all due to the social pressures through advertising, movies and various other social media, where they have created ideas of who we should be, and what we should dress like and look like to be socially acceptable. The biggest question that has remained unanswered for decades now is: Who set the standards for a personality type and who judges that personality type, against what criteria?

Should one have been labeled as a Personality type and one does not meet that criterion, whatever that criterion may be, it will definitely have a negative influence on your level of success in your life. In order to live a fulfilled lifestyle follow your passions and dreams and do not let anyone persuade you into believing that you have to comply with others opinions and beliefs in order to fulfill the role as a personality type.

Chapter- eight

Golden Tactics for Manipulation

We talk about people being manipulative and are often irritated by them for these behaviors or we have a vague sense that others have manipulated us, but what is the real definition of manipulation?

The definition of manipulation: Using clever and devious ways to control or influence somebody or something, to change by artful or unfair means, and serving one's own purpose. All that to put it in a polite way that due to your self-serving or self-centered motives, you try to get someone else to do something for you that you probably can do for yourself; you just do not want to do it.

For other people, there can be a smug satisfaction in getting over on people and having others do things for them that they are more than capable of doing.

The clues one can look for in your own or other's manipulation is about how is the request stated, the posture used when asking, and sometimes the specific words used. There are generally self-serving attitudes present in manipulation:

Scheming - To have somebody do something or get out of something

Calculating – Conniving, devious or dishonest

Controlling - Crafty, Wily and sly

Manipulation is one's personally motivated short-term agenda that does not consider others except how you can use them. Learning what your preferred method of manipulation is important if you want to stop this behavior. You are probably very good at your method. One can no longer throw oneself on the floor, kick and scream as you did when you were two, however, you may still use tears as a ploy.

You may not do the "Please, Oh Please" of the adolescent girl, but you continue asking and asking and asking until finally someone breaks down and does it for you.

Anger also gets people's attention and people feel uncomfortable around it. Therefore, people may give in and eventually let you have your way thus changing the mood.

There are causes that tug at our heartstrings as well - donating to small children and puppies can give you a warm fuzzy feeling. However, do you find that you are more inclined to give to these causes and not other needy organizations or groups of people because they do not have a photogenic or compelling front person?

Manipulative Methods

When confronted about a behavior, my drug or alcohol use, or not keeping a promise, one pretends to be helpless, play the victim incompetent, or make statements on being " stupid " or " dumb " or statements that indicate other people should feel sorry for them for their lack of experience, education, awareness or support.

I say, "Anything you want", "You're right", or "I'll get on it", when I mean it not. I am doing this to placate someone or get him or her to quit talking about the problems I have created.

I act depressed especially in the midst of selective people and then "magically" appear okay around others.

I "butter it up or suck it up" to people; not actually meaning the words but hoping that I can get something out of them.

I use guilt - statements like, "You made it ", "Your family encourages you", "You got a good education", "You were and are not abused", "I wasn't validated as a teenager", etc.

One does not get what they want and then try to reframe the request in a different way so that others are responsible for me and give me what I want.

When you use these types of manipulative behaviors or statements, you are usually trying to get others to feel guilty or obligated to you to get you what you want, get out of some of the responsibility, or in some cases, to simply get some attention.

Learn to call these kinds of behaviors and postures what they are; choosing to act a certain way to get predictable results. Claiming stupidity or incompetence generally moves the conversation from what you are doing or not doing to the fact that you are not stupid or dumb.

It distracts the other participant in the conversation and then you do not have to stay focused on their criticism of what you were doing or not doing. It usually works in your favor. If one is too incompetent to do something, then obviously someone else will have to do it for you.

This can then set up another issue. Each time your manipulation works, you start believing your own lies. You have created some of these images - stupid, worthless, helpless, incompetent, or underprivileged. Those labels become the cost one pays for what one gets from others.

The Price of Using Guilt to Manipulate Others

When one is manipulating to get someone's needs or wants to be satisfied using guilt, one runs the risk of eventually alienating people. These people may resent you in the end when they eventually realize that you are in a position to do that which they did for you.

Owning your Self-Serving Motive

An ideal way to deal with this issue is honesty with others and yourself. Owning that one has a motive that is self-serving in the request that may not always sound like an alternative that is the best. Nevertheless, one's honesty may prove refreshing to others. People might be inclined to help more. However, with an honest request, they are helping and not a manipulative request.

A working rule of the thumb is used to assess the self-serving motive percentage in your actions and requests. Giving people an opportunity to help you means that they if they choose to help, they may feel proud or needed in the exchange, so they are receiving something from your request, as well as you getting help.

Health professionals have raised concerns in recent times, about the lack of nutritional information in the community. Could this be one reason for the plethora of food shows now seen on television? How much of what we see on the small screen, can be believed? Are we being manipulated by our choice of foods and being educated in nutrition, without really being aware of it? In 2011, an Australian pioneer in celebrity cooking, Margaret Fulton, slammed contestants and judges alike, in the series, "My Kitchen Rules" and "Master-Chef" as not knowing even the basic things like "making pastry" and "doing everything wrong."

The legitimacy of argument

Fulton's blast at the popular shows raises a couple of interesting points. The shows "Master-Chef" and "My Kitchen Rules," were sponsored at the time, by Coles. Fulton had just launched a campaign for a rival group, Woolworths, which raises the point of just how legitimate were her responses to these two television shows. It matters not, whether her complaints about the two shows were in fact, correct in her opinion. The fact that she was working with a food production rival, places her observations at risk.

Manipulation has no doubt, been a factor ever since people assumed power over others. We are manipulated every waking moment with a barrage of advertising, fact and opinion, in order that we comply with the wants and needs of the purveyor of that advertising. I am attempting to persuade you right now, which is a form of manipulation, in order that you bear witness to my opinion. The art of persuasion is a fact and we use that form, whenever we participate in a normal conversation. Manipulation is more aggressive in its result, rather than its form.

Manipulation or persuasion?

Quite often, we do not even realize that we are being manipulated, until we become conscious of the change in our attitude or ideas regarding a subject. Our defenses were down and we probably had no inkling of the mind changing form of persuasion that was being aimed at us. During persuasion, I listen to your point of view and I am able to decide, on a conscious level, whether I want to agree or whether I have a different point of view, but if I am being manipulated, then quite likely I do not realize the change in attitude that is being applied. If I was not aware that Margaret Fulton had agreed to launch a program for Woolworths, for example, I may have been impressed by her argument that Matt Preston was more showman than chef, however with the knowledge that she may have had conflicting interests for her outburst, lessened the impact of her statement for me.

We are influenced at all times by advertising, opinion, and even conversation and it is often difficult to see the manipulation of our thinking. We want to believe we are in control of our own thoughts.

Ask ourselves are we really? There are often hidden agendas and it is awareness of those influences that assist us to be either willing pawns or not, in the game of life.

Chapter nine

Golden Tactics for Persuasion

The Art of Persuasion is conceivably the most important thing a person can learn because success or failure often is dependent upon our capability to communicate with other people. Oftentimes in life, whom you know is more important than what you know.

People often experience a common obstacle while they try to get good at The Art of Persuasion because many persuasive techniques being taught are simply not reliable. In fact, it is not uncommon for people to spend time and money in learning persuasive techniques that are not successful in helping them achieve their goals. A major example of this is when people study Ericksonian hypnosis with the hopes of increasing their sales and getting better jobs. Ericksonian hypnosis is for therapeutic purposes only, and has absolutely nothing to do with The Art of Persuasion.

It is only the disguised types of hypnosis that contain the persuasive techniques that give you results outside of clinical settings. For centuries, the invisible styles of mind control hypnosis being practiced by world leaders and politicians. This means that if powerful persuasive techniques can be practiced on large scales such as leadership and politics, that you can also use persuasive techniques on smaller scales such as work environments and personal relationships.

Your work environment can provide you with money, resources, and benefits, so your work environment is an important area where you should be implementing your persuasive techniques. As you elevate your status at your workplace, you will also elevate your status in every other place that you are a part of. The more skillful you get at mastering the skills of The Art of Persuasion, the more promotions and doors there will be that will open for you.
The Art of Persuasion is not only an art but also a science. The persuasive techniques of persuasion are powerful and if they are applied appropriately, you will get steady results from using them. Persuasive

techniques have also been scientifically verified to enrich people's relationships because when the art of persuasion is used for good, you can convince people to make better decisions so that they can live better lives.

There is, however, one regularly overlooked part of The Art of Persuasion that not too many people know about, and this is the philosophy of defensive persuasion. What defensive persuasion does is give you the skill to defend against the dishonesty of others who are attempting to covertly persuade you in the direction of choices that are not in your best interest. Most trainers agree that defensive persuasion is far more imperative than the usual persuasive techniques that focus on what to do to others instead of how to defend yourself.

One thing is if there was just one thing in life, if there was only one hobby that you should become skilled at, it is without a doubt The Art of Persuasion.

Persuasive skills can be learned through failure. The most critical part of failure understanding is via defining it. Failure is defined by giving up on the persuasive process or just winging it without a game plan. Failure can also be defined by not making it even though you did everything you were supposed to do but do everything afterward to determine why the persuasion was not made. Either way you define failure persuasive techniques require structure and scripting to your process.

The fear of failure has stopped more people before they have even started than most other reasons. It is the same reason that people keep working in a job that they hate year after year. Many times entrepreneurs will say the best thing that happened to them is that they were fired or lost a job that caused them to perform for a new function. You will battle failure in either definition as long as you work on your persuasive abilities.

So what exactly does this have to do with persuasion success? Failure in some aspect or another is not only normal it is to be expected over time. Even the best people in most industries close at only 70%, which means that they fail 30% of the time or did them. Do you think that it bothers a person to walk away from a speech? This question probably is their focus long after their persuasive speech even though they have let the pain of losing. They always want to know how to increase their persuasion skills.

The mistake is to let another person define what a persuasive failure is to you in so much as they can tell you that you are a failure. Plenty of successful people still make silly mistakes every day they have just lost focus on what they know works or they have gotten lazy.

Failure can be of benefit to you as a person by finding out what does not work and what does.

What may work for a coworker or another person does not mean that it will work for you and that is OK. Sales success comes from you finding out what works for you. Persuasive skills for each person may be different depending upon their abilities and or demeanor. This is actually great news because you may be able to find persuasive skills to dominate in your marketplace that others cannot. This also explains why you have seen or heard other people do things that you cannot duplicate even though you have tried.

Success is a mystery for some because they allow it to be. For you to gain persuasive abilities sometimes you will have to fail and be all right with that. If you are scared of success, you will not find yourself having it.

There is at some point where you have to be vulnerable and even seen as vulnerable to grow in just about every aspect of your life. Sometimes being vulnerable means asking for help, failing or even not succeeding at the level that you want and or desire as soon or as fast as desired.

There are people who will get to a point where they think that they have failed. This is silly also because as a person there will always be a project that does not go through. Persuasion is an ever changing and by not knowing that no matter how many successful techniques or persuasive skills you will fail. You are industry if it has not changed yet it will soon. That is just how business is evolution is part of every job or industry.

Chapter ten

Golden Tactics for Deception

Since the fertility until birth, everything is designed and created using a predetermined program. The basis of creation is on reality and facts so that human being should understand the existence and its purpose. The human life progressed and propagated on a straight and right path with justification as the foundation is laid on truth. However, the diversion in life leads into a disaster if human beings adopt lies and continue in the deceptive realm. It is obligatory that we all should explore and understand what is truth, lies and deception.

The truth is defined as, "The state of being in accord with a particular fact or reality. It is in accord with the body of real things, events or actualities." Many scholars and philosophers are continuing to debate various theories regarding truth; its logical, factual and ethical meanings. However, its literal and structural meaning are in unison expressing the executions of facts in action and deeds. Therefore, in this materialistic society, it is expressed as a bitter pill. On the other hand, its intrinsic value is bliss and satisfaction.

The world has witnessed, on many occasions, the reward it attaches to the truthful people. Their words are recognized as gospel truth. These people are termed as trustworthy and dependable. An authentic but an indisputable fact is that telling truth restricts one's action and deeds to factuality. However, the lies are covering up and substantiating falsehood by lying repeatedly. Hence, we need to explore the meaning of lies and its effects.

A lie from definition; Is a false statement made with deliberate intent to deceive. It is also an intentional untruth or falsehood." The definition is self-explanatory and needs no emphasis. However, the reasons, circumstances and situational demands do compel individuals to commit to telling lies. This act will lead to disastrous consequences resulting in tarnishing an image and collapse of a system.

The discussion about lying may substantiate technically in favor of a person telling lies depending upon his own concept. Consequently, it will give a temporary recess yet it will doom defeat. Finally, the factuality will emerge and reveal the person's trust and worthiness. The situational lies may appear logical, and appropriate still an aura of deception prevails in a disguised form. It is advisable to explore deception too. The nuance of deception is best understood along with lies.

The deception is closely associated with lies and finely woven within its concept and meaning. The motivation is a principal cause of deception. It could be between two individual or groups and nations. The variance of deception can be romantic, cultural, corporate and political. The purpose is to camouflage the motive and present it as an acceptable solution to achieve the ultimately predetermined aim.

There is a marked difference between truth alone and truth bias. When the truth becomes bias presenting relational transgression at the cost of the factuality of events then lies, and deception gets camouflage. Therefore, it is advisable to restrict ourselves or adhere to the core concept of truth, within its sanctity. When situational demands exceed its limit and is emphasizing truth bias then the reality of events are relegated. It influences the minds of the decision maker affecting negatively the recipient. He then becomes the victim of circumstances, yelling and pleading for mercy on the deaf ears. A nuance between factuality and motives can become deceptive if lies are camouflage. Thereby, a conscious approach should be adopted differentiating between, truth, lies and deception to avoid injustice.

You may believe that it is perfectly OK to deceive another person because you have been hurt. Sooner or later that deception will cause you harm in one form or another. Often you may find that the biggest deception that you are taking part in is the one against yourself. If you are constantly deceiving, yourself and personal progress can be difficult.

The desire to make personal progress is something that must be boring inside your heart. If you are constantly frustrated with the way in which other people argue you think you will eventually become disenchanted with all of the humanity. Instead, you can focus on your ability to be as honest as possible so that the interactions you have with other people are as honest as possible.

Honesty can build bridges when it comes to helping other people understand your perceptions and perspective. When you see, all understood you are more likely to be honest with others. Honesty also creates the opportunity for solutions that can be created for the enhancement of everyone involved. When you feel that you can enhance the lives of others you will be able to creatively solve any challenges you were facing in the past.

Sometimes emotionally, dealing with things can be very difficult. If your emotions are not properly developed you will feel as though you are being punished when that is not the case. Avoiding this punishment will all but cause you to be dishonest with yourself when what you are dealing with has you emotionally and physically drained. Identifying ways to relieve your stress is necessary so you can continue to be productive.

Productivity also is helpful when trying to identify ways in which things can change to improve your situation. If you are not able to deal with the truth as it currently has been focused on the ways in which you want things to change. When you have any belief that things can change for your best interests you will then also have the strength to see that things can be changed radically.

Identifying the areas where you were lying to yourself is one of the most important things that you can do to improve the quality of your life. Your life is something that is constantly evolving and therefore you must think about the ways in which of these deceptions are not helping you to reach your overall objectives. The constant reevaluation of your objectives is something that you must consider in the end.

Conclusion

Any parent can tell you that using reverse psychology works for almost any situation requiring a little extra boost in motivation for their child. It could be as simple as telling him that you want his vegetables at dinner or that you want to wear his shirt when he doesn't get dressed, to as complex as packing his suitcase when he says he wants to run away. When used appropriately and cautiously, this form of reasoning works almost every time.

What is reverse psychology? Simply stated, it some form of mild manipulation that encourages someone to do the opposite of what he thinks you want him to. It is not only effective with children, but it can also be used in dating and relationships, business, and sales. The reason this approach is so effective is that it taps into the natural defiance mechanism of humans. If you tell a child to eat his string beans, for instance, he will most likely flat out refuse. If you tell him not to eat his string beans because you want them more, he will probably eat every last one on his plate.

In business, using reverse psychology can be effective as well. Instead of asking an employee to perform a task he doesn't want to do, try telling him that you know the task might be hard for him because he is too busy and that you are thinking of giving it to someone else. In this case, the employee will probably decide to accomplish the task because you have indirectly told him you do not think he can, and most adults do not want someone else to get credit for accomplishing work that was first offered to them.

Even in dating situations, reverse psychology can bring about changes in the relationship. If the object of your affections is playing hard to get, making him or her believe you did not want them to start with will likely drive the person right back to you by feeding into his or her dislike of rejection. Agreeing to remain just friends is another way to make him or her rethink her actions.

There are some important things to remember if you plan on using reverse psychology. The first is that you never want to go overboard and make someone feel less valuable as a human. Telling your child that the shirt you want him to wear would not look good on him anyway is one example of being too harsh using this method. Telling him instead that you want to wear the shirt yourself will bring about better results without damaging his self-esteem. Telling your employee that he is just not capable of performing the task would be another step too far when using reverse psychology.

The second thing to keep in mind is that you cannot change methods in mid-negotiation. You must quickly size up your approach and choose reverse psychology from the start to get the results you want. You cannot beg your potential boyfriend or girlfriend to remain with you and then suddenly start using reverse psychology; this will not be effective in achieving your goals. Likewise, once you start using this approach, it is hard to effectively stop and switch to a different method to get results.

While not always successful you will usually find that when you are faced with difficult situations and personalities, you are more likely to achieve desired results by using reverse psychology to achieve your goals as long as it is done gently and appropriately.

Thank you for choosing to read this book. I believe it has been helpful in helping you in your reverse psychology skills.

Made in the USA
Las Vegas, NV
18 March 2024

87386355R10056